# "IN THEIR OWN WORDS"

# MEDIEVAL TIMES

Robert Hull

## W
## FRANKLIN WATTS
### LONDON • SYDNEY

First published in 2001 by
Franklin Watts
96 Leonard Street
EC2A 4XD

Franklin Watts Australia
56 O'Riordan Street
Alexandria
NS W 2015

Series editor: Rachel Cooke
Editor: Sarah Ridley
Designer: Jason Anscomb
Consultant: Dr Sandra Raban, Fellow in
Medieval History, Trinity Hall, Cambridge
Illustrations: Mike White
Cover images: The British Library, London/
AKG London: front & back covers bl & br.
Whilst every attempt has been made to clear
copyright should there be an inadvertent
omission please apply in the first instance to
the publisher regarding rectification.

A CIP catalogue record for this book
is available from the British Library.

ISBN 0 7496 4069 3

Dewey Classification 942.03

Printed in Malaysia

# "IN THEIR OWN WORDS"

# Introduction

## Medieval Times 1066-1485

When historians refer to the term 'medieval', they mean the period of time from the invasion of England by William the Conqueror in 1066 to the start of Tudor times, about 1485. People at the time would not have referred to themselves as medieval – but the term is useful when analysing this period of history. Great changes took place during these five hundred years, so it is perhaps easier to imagine this huge period of time if we divide it up into three smaller parts.

### 1066-1204

Saxon kingship ended in 1066, with the defeat of King Harold at the Battle of Hastings. The winner, William, Duke of Normandy, secured the throne of England for himself and the Norman Conquest began. From this date until 1204, when King John lost the Duchy of Normandy, the kings of England mainly lived in France. Even beyond 1204, these kings were Frenchmen, thinking and speaking French, and replacing English with French as the language of court and government.

In order to control the land in their absence, the kings ordered many castles to be built. By 1100, at least five hundred castles had been constructed using earthworks and wooden buildings to provide defensive positions. These castles and the land and power that went with them, were given to the French nobles[1] in return for military service and homage[2]. This trade of land for services dominated everyone's life at the time. It is often referred to as the feudal system[3].

### 1204-1348

By now the kings of England had less territory in France so they spent more time in England. There was a country to govern, barons to control, and rebellions to prevent.

There always seemed to be wars. English kings fought to rule Scotland, Wales and Ireland. They sent Crusaders to fight against Muslim Arab armies and Christian heretics[4], or actually fought on Crusades themselves.

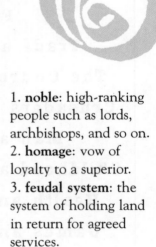

1. **noble**: high-ranking people such as lords, archbishops, and so on.
2. **homage**: vow of loyalty to a superior.
3. **feudal system**: the system of holding land in return for agreed services.

4. **heretic**: someone who goes against the accepted religious beliefs.

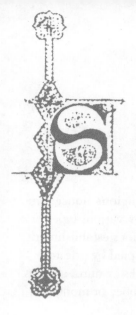

Kings lived in a world of kings, watching out for their thrones, marrying for power, making laws, controlling the barons and endlessly travelling. But many medieval people were bound to one lord, living their lives in one village.

So everyday life, farming, crafts and trade, went on alongside war and politics. Ships carried wool, the main export, to Flanders in Belgium, and coal from the north-east of England to London. Towns grew up, immigrant workers arrived and brought their crafts with them. Parliament developed as kings discovered they needed the co-operation of barons, churchmen and the wealthy to raise money.

England became multilingual, with English spoken in the streets, French in the law courts and Latin amongst travelling churchmen and diplomats. Official documents and public writing, records of courts and most letters, were in Latin. Many English dialects were spoken, to the extent that some English people couldn't understand each other: 'All the languages of the Northumbrians, and especially at York, is so sharp, cutting, and abrasive, that we southerners can scarcely understand that language,' wrote Ranulph Higden in the early 14th century.

## 1348-1500

The middle period of medieval times ended in 1348 when a terrible plague, the Black Death, probably killed at least a third of the population. Life was changed forever for those who survived and the feudal system gradually began to break down. Many villages were deserted and, with a great shortage of labourers and craftsmen, people found themselves better able to make a good living. There was grumbling discontent against the rich and powerful and, in 1381, the Peasants' Revolt broke out.

But even amongst all this, only thirty or so years after the Black Death, the poet Geoffrey Chaucer's *Canterbury Tales* gives us pictures of comfortable good living; of a well-dressed cloth-merchant's wife travelling endlessly on pilgrimages; of a monk who hunts most of the time; and of a hospitable steward whose house 'snowed meat and drink'.

We might feel we know Chaucer's people. But in many ways this later period of the medieval era is still like a distant country. People had no ready-made clothes, no quick methods of travel, no ways of keeping most food fresh. We might also find strange the laws they obeyed and broke, the way illnesses were treated, the things they believed. The medieval world was a religious world, full of belief and superstition, and of religious houses[1], many with large estates.

## Medieval Voices

Medieval times seem less strange when we overhear the 'voices' of the people. Monks, chroniclers[2], poets and even family letters have survived, telling us, for instance, how pleased a 15th-century mother was that her son was well 'belashed' by his master at Cambridge! We also have laws, treaties, land deeds, household accounts, and of course the Domesday Book, all of which give details about life at this time.

Yet most medieval people didn't write and read, especially women, so we only hear the words of these people when someone else reports them. Those we do hear directly are the educated – mainly Church people or fairly wealthy types.

Some of the words we hear were written in English, an English we can just about read, despite the spelling and many different words. But most writing – the histories or 'chronicles' of the times, the court records, all official letters, and before 1400, most personal ones too – was in Latin. So we hear all those voices in translations from Latin, or from medieval English.

However, some words just can't be translated. These are the technical words like 'fief' that have mostly gone out of English now. These are explained in footnotes. Sometimes, where a piece is very short and the meaning seems obvious, or where it is from a poem, we have given the actual medieval English, and only modernized the spelling.

1. **religious house**: one of the various types of religious establishment occupied by priests, monks or nuns, such as an abbey or monastery.

2. **chronicler**: one who records events, a kind of early historian.

6

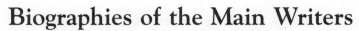

# Biographies of the Main Writers

**Baha'ad-Din** (1145-1234) entered the service of Saladin in 1188 as a judge or Qadi, and went on to write the story of his life, reporting much of it as an eye-witness.

**Geoffrey Chaucer** (1345-1400) is the most famous poet of medieval times, whose best-known work, *Canterbury Tales*, recounts the stories told by pilgrims travelling to Canterbury.

**William Fitzstephen** died about 1190. He was chaplain to Thomas Becket when Becket was Henry II's Chancellor and wrote a *History of Thomas Becket*.

**Jean Froissart** (c.1377-1410) was a Frenchman at the court of Edward III. He travelled around Britain, and his *Chroniques* cover the period between about 1325 and 1400.

**Gerald of Wales** (1146-1220) was the son of a Welsh princess who studied in Paris. He wrote books about a journey through Wales, the history of Wales, and others.

**Jocelin of Brakelond** was a monk of the Abbey at Bury St Edmunds. His *Chronicle* covering the years 1173-1202 is a fascinating picture of everyday medieval life, and an admiring portrait of his abbot, Samson.

**Henry Knighton**, a late 14th-century canon of Leicester Abbey, wrote a history called *Chronicon* covering the years from 959 to 1395, with detailed accounts of the Black Death and the Peasants' Revolt.

**William Langland** (c. 1330-c. 1400) was a Midlands based poet, known from his poem *The Vision of Piers Plowman*.

**The Paston family** lived in Norfolk, in the village of Paston. Their numerous letters to each other across three generations give a vivid picture of fairly well-off English life during the Wars of the Roses.

**William of Malmesbury** (died c. 1143) was a librarian of Malmesbury Abbey. He wrote books on the history of England between 440-1142.

**Thomas Walsingham** saw the Peasants' Revolt and the 1383 'crusade' to France at first hand, and recorded those events in *Chronicon Angliae*, which covers from 1328-1388.

# Kings, Queens and Nobles

From 1066 the English were ruled by 'foreigners', namely Frenchmen who continued to hold lands in France as dukes and counts. They spoke French, and, until 1331, swore homage[1] to the kings of France.

1. **homage**: see page 4.

Perhaps in a strange way this helped England to develop. Absent kings sometimes tried to make sure that while they were away from England, government went on as usual. Under Henry II law courts sat more regularly and more written records were kept.

Towards the end of the medieval era, the Wars of the Roses broke out between families descended from two sons of Edward III (died 1377). One brother was the Duke of Lancaster, the other Duke of York. The quarrel about who should rule England became a war that dragged on for forty years. In the end, England was reunited by the Tudor family.

## The Norman Kings

Ralph, the Abbot of Coggeshall from 1207-18, described the link between Normandy and kings of England in his journals.

*From Duke William, who conquered the kingdom of the English, down to King John, who lost the duchy and many other lands across the sea in the fifth year of his reign, the kings of England had always been dukes of Normandy, holding the duchy and the kingdom together for 139 years.*

Ralph, Abbot of Coggeshall, c. 1210

## Feudal Kingship

The Kings of England governed their land through the feudal system of land-holding in return for services. The king was at the top of this social order and his nobles[2], his vassals[3], swore homage to their king, which meant that they promised to provide their lord with services, especially as knights in wartime, in return for land. The most powerful churchmen were on the same level as the nobles. Here William I demands armed knights from the Abbot of Evesham in 1072:

2. **noble**: see page 4.
3. **vassal**: someone who held land from a lord in return for vows of homage and service.

*I command you to summon all those within your jurisdiction to bring to my presence all the knights they owe me, in a state of readiness, at Clarendon a week after Whitsun. You too should come before me on that day and bring with you those five knights that you owe me from your abbey, likewise in a state of readiness.*

Royal writ to the Abbot of Evesham, 1072

The idea of homage explains why kings, and all lords, expected services from their vassals. Here, in 1127, Galbert of Bruges, writing in *De Multro... Karolis Comitis Flandiarum*, describes how Count William Clito of Flanders gave a fief[4] to tenants in return for 'the obligations of their homage':

4. **fief**: land held in return for military service.

*They did homage in this way. The Count asked the vassal if he wished to become his man, without any reservation, and the man said, "I do." The man put his hands together, and placed them in the hands of the Count. They then pledged themselves to each other with a kiss. The man who had performed his homage then pledged loyalty to the Count, saying, "I promise by my faith to be loyal to the Count, and to fulfil the obligations of my homage completely, in good faith, without deceitfulness, against all men," and he made this vow on the saint's relics... The Count, with a small stick that he held, invested with their fiefs all who had done homage and taken the oath.*

Galbert of Bruges, 1127

## The Succession

The medieval period was troubled by many quarrels over the succession, meaning securing the throne for the next king or queen. Fights broke out, some of which led to civil wars. A son of Henry II (king 1154-1189) explains the quarrels in their family, in a chronicle by Roger of Howden.

*Do you not know that it is our nature, planted in us by inheritance from our ancestors, that none of us should love*

*the other, but that always, brother against brother and son against father, we try our utmost to injure each other?*

Roger of Howden, c. 1190

Succession problems continued through the medieval period. In 1327 Edward II was pushed off the throne by his own wife, and her lover. Then, in 1399, Richard II was removed from his throne by a conspiracy, as described by his supporter, Richard Dreux. Here the Earl of Northumberland – who is in league with Bolingbroke, Duke of Lancaster, the future Henry IV – leads Richard II into an ambush:

*"My lord," said the Earl, "I will go on ahead and order your supper, and tell my lord the Duke what I have done."*
*The Earl then left, taking the seven attendants who had come with him, and rode ahead to where he had left his men waiting on the mountainside, ready for the ambush. They were cheered to hear him say, "We shall soon have what we have been looking for."*
*In the meantime King Richard, who had no idea of the villainy and treason the Earl had been brewing up, remounted with his men – only twelve of them – and started on his way again. Then as he and his men were riding down the side of the mountain, they saw the Earl of Northumberland's men, armed, waiting below in the valley. Richard said to the Earl of Salisbury, "Can you see banners and streamers down there in the valley?"*
*The Earl said, "I can, my lord, I smell trouble."*
*"I suspect that man has betrayed you," the Bishop of Carlisle said. He had no sooner said this than the Earl of Northumberland appeared with 12 men and rode up to them...*
*"Northumberland," said the King, "if I thought you wanted to betray me, I would turn back to Conway."*
*"By St George, my lord, you are not going back there for a month at least; I shall escort you to my lord the Duke of Lancaster, as I promised him."*

Richard Dreux, c. 1410.

# Domesday Book

The best kings were keen to govern well, as is shown by William the Conqueror's determination to find out in detail about the country he had conquered. In 1085, he ordered commissioners to make a report of all the land and possessions in England. It took a year to complete.

The Domesday Book gives a detailed view of life in the 11th century, naming thousands of towns and villages although not all. Here is an extract from the 'Inquest' for Ely:

*Here follows how the manor[1] is called; who held it in the time of Edward the Confessor; who holds it now; how many hides[2] there are; how many plough teams on the demesne[3]; how many villeins[4]; how may cottars[5]; how many slaves[6]; how many freemen[7]; how many socmen[8]; how much woodland; how much pasture; how many mills; how many fishponds; how much all was worth then; how much now. All this in triplicate.*

Domesday Book, 1086

The writer of the *Anglo-Saxon Chronicle* for 1085 was indignant at this prying survey.

*Not a single hide – it's shameful to say, though he was not ashamed to do it – not a yard of land, not one ox, cow, or pig was left out from what was recorded.*

Anglo-Saxon Chronicle, 1085

# The King's Power

Kings often had difficulty with their barons, bishops and abbots. Henry II's son, Richard I (1189-1199) only spent about 6 months of his 10-year reign in England, being mainly interested in war and Crusades. It didn't make him popular with his barons. He is supposed to have said:

*If I could have found a buyer, I would have sold London itself.*

Richard I, c. 1190

1. **manor**: a feudal estate of manor house and fields, with its own manor court.
2. **hide**: a land measurement – approx. 120 acres.
3. **demesne**: the lord's home farm which could be scattered among his tenants' land.
4. **villein**: a peasant farmer whose land belonged to the lord.
5. **cottars**: cottagers.
6. **slaves**: an unpaid labourer or servant legally bound to a lord.
7. **freemen**: men not legally bound to the manor.
8. **socmen**: men under the lord's legal jurisdiction who only paid rent for their land – no services.

Samson, Abbot of Bury St Edmunds Priory, resisted the king's demands, as Jocelin, a monk there, describes in his chronicle of the years 1173-1202.

*King Richard ordered his bishops and abbots to make sure that one knight out of every ten in their lands was to join him in Normandy, bringing horses and weapons, to support him in his battles against the French King. The abbot himself was expected to send four knights. But when his knights arrived in answer to a summons, they said that the lands they held from St Edmund did not demand knight service outside England. They had never gone abroad on knight service, neither had their fathers, though sometimes, on the orders of the king, they had paid scutage[1]. The abbot was put in a difficult position. On one hand there was a clear threat to the independence of his knights; on the other, he was worried that he might lose possession of his own lands if he failed to perform his service to the king.*

Jocelin, c. 1202

1. **scutage**: a money payment to the king to avoid military service.

By 1215, the power of the king of England was being questioned by his barons and earls. They wanted the rights of the nobles[2] and the Church to be written in law so that, for instance, the king had to ask their permission before raising more taxes. The long document of 63 clauses, the Magna Carta, that King John was forced to accept, eventually led to the development of Parliament.

2. **nobles**: see page 4.

*To secure the common agreement of the realm for imposing an aid ... we undertake to send sealed letters to summon archbishops, bishops, abbots, earls and greater barons, and we shall also summon all those who hold land directly from us ... and in the letters we shall clearly state the reason for the summons.*

In some clauses, important ideas about people's freedom and rights were expressed.

3. **sheriff**: the king's representative in a county with wide ranging legal powers.
4. **freeman**: see page 11.

*No town or person shall be forced to build bridges over rivers except those who always had to do so.*
*No sheriff[3] or royal official or anyone else shall take horses or carts for transport from any freeman, without his consent.*
*No man shall be forced to perform more service for a knight's fee than is due from it.*
*No freeman[4] shall be seized or imprisoned or stripped of his rights or possessions or outlawed or exiled, or deprived of his standing in any way, nor shall we use force against him, except by the lawful judgement of his equals or by the law of the land.*

Magna Carta, 1215

By the late 13th century, kings wanting money for wars discussed matters with Parliament or their chief subjects. Henry V made this speech to important Londoners in 1415:
*We intend with no small army to visit parts beyond the sea, to reconquer the lands that are part of what the heir to this realm expects… In order that we can make arrangements for borrowing a satisfactory sum of money … we have decided, knowing that you will readily fall in with our wishes, especially since the purpose of our project will result in obvious benefit to the whole kingdom, to send certain Lords from our Council to the City, to discuss and negotiate with you about the whole business.*

Henry V, 1415

# Warfare and Disorder

English kings were constantly at war. They fought for power over Scotland, Wales or Ireland and they were always fighting in France. King after king of England campaigned in France, to defend or add to the lands they held there. From 1337, when Edward III claimed the French throne for himself, until 1453 there were a series of wars known as the Hundred Years' War, between France and England. Yet by 1455 England had lost all its French lands except Calais.

War was normal – a normal way of settling disputes, and for the knight, a way of life. Medieval times were violent, with most people carrying a weapon of some sort. Even churchmen fought.

## Medieval War

In some ways, medieval war meant life as usual – for the rich. Jean Froissart describes Edward III marching towards Paris in 1360, the year a peace treaty was signed.

*You ought to know that the King of England and the rich brought with them on their carts, tents, pavilions, mills, cooking ovens, horse-smithies and everything needful. And to furnish this they brought along quite six thousand carts, each with four good strong cart-horses brought out of England. And on the carts they carried boats, so cleverly made out of boiled leather that it was surprising to see them. They could carry three men so as to float on the biggest lake or fish-pond and fish at will. Thus they were quite comfortable in Lent[1] – that is to say the lords and people of standing. But the common folk had to make do with what they could get.*

Jean Froissart, c. 1360

1. **Lent**: the forty days before Easter, when Christians traditionally fast.

Churchmen sometimes fought, though they were not supposed to. In 1070 the Norman bishops imposed penances[2] on soldiers and churchmen for killings done in war.

*Anyone who knows that he killed a man in the great battle*

2. **penance**: an act undertaken to show sorrow for a sin.

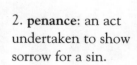

14

*[Hastings] must do penance ... for each man that he killed... The clerics[3] who fought, or who were armed to fight, must do penance as if they had committed these sins in their own country; because church law forbids them to fight in battles.*

Bishop of Sitten, 1070

3. **clerics**: men of the Church.

The technology of war changed when Welsh archers fought at the Battle of Agincourt in France, 1415. This battle was part of the English kings' continuing struggle for the throne of France. A nobleman of Artois, Jehan de Wavrin, made this comment in his *Chronicle*.

*The French were so loaded with armour that they could not support themselves or move forward. In the first place they were armed with long coats of steel, reaching to the knees or lower, and very heavy, over the leg harness, and besides plate armour most of them had hooded helmets. With all this weight of armour, and the softness of the ground, it kept them as if immoveable, so that it was only with great difficulty that they could raise their clubs...*

*The English archers ... began to send their arrows on the French with great vigour. The archers mostly in their doublets[4], without armour, their stockings rolled up to their knees, with hatchets or battle-axes or great swords hung from their belts. Some were bare-footed and bare-headed.*

Jehan de Wavrin, 15th century

4. **doublet**: a close-fitting jacket.
5. **pillagers**: ones who pillage, that is loot and steal.

Massacres happened in medieval war. When the Bishop of Limoges changed from supporting the English to the French in 1370, Edward III's son, the Black Prince, took a horrible revenge, as described in Froissart's *Chronicle*.

*You would have seen pillagers[5], bent on doing harm, running through the town, killing men, women and children... It was a terrible, sad sight, every rank and age of person throwing themselves on their knees in front of the prince and begging for mercy. But he was so crazed with fury and the thirst for vengeance that he listened to no-one. Everyone was slaughtered, even the most innocent, wherever they were found. I do not know why the poor were not left unharmed. They were not involved in the bishop's treachery, but they still suffered... More than three thousand men, women and children were put to death that day.*

Jean Froissart, c. 1400

Despite all this, a French writer, Honoré Bonet, thought war was a good thing.

*War is not an evil thing. It is a valuable, good thing, because by its very nature it only tries to put right what is wrong, and make peace where there are quarrels. And even if evil things are done during a war, those things aren't part of the true nature of war; they happen when war is perverted in some way.*

Honoré Bonet, end of 14th century

# War round Britain

Kings of England wanted to control Scotland, Wales and Ireland. In 1092 William Rufus used an army to drive out the ruler of Cumberland, who ruled the land for Malcolm, King of Scotland, as described in the *Anglo-Saxon Chronicle*.

*He went north to Carlisle with a great army and there he restored the town and then built a castle. He drove out Dolfin, the previous ruler of that land, and garrisoned[1] the castle with his own men before returning south. He sent many peasants there with their wives and livestock to live there and cultivate the land.*

Anglo-Saxon Chronicle, 1092

1. **garrisoned:** occupied with soldiers.

Fierce wars between England and Scotland started in the reign of Edward I (1272-1307). The Scots won a great victory at Bannockburn in 1314, described in the *Chronicle of Lanercost.*

*Another calamity happened to the English. They had crossed a wide stream called Bannockburn, into which the tide flows, and now they wanted to re-cross it. In the crush and confusion many nobles[2] and others fell into the stream with their horses; others, with great difficulty, struggled out of it, but many were never able to extricate themselves. Bannockburn was spoken about for many years by the English.*

Chronicle of Lanercost, 14th century

2. **nobles:** see page 4.

In 1328 England agreed to respect Scotland's independence. But fighting still went on, and the English captured King David Bruce in 1347 and held him for ransom. Henry Knighton wrote a chronicle at the end of the 14th century, describing what happened in 1348.

*Then the Scots came to redeem David, their king. They were told that they would have to provide compensation for the harm they had done to the king of England and to the kingdom before that time and then they could have their king redeemed. The Scots hurried home and gathered their forces, and made raids on England, devastating the countryside, burning towns, slaying people and capturing many sleeping in their beds, taking them off to Scotland and setting impossible ransom amounts.*

*So the English, with the idea of enticing the Scots into England, proclaimed a tournament at Berwick. The Scots travelled to the tournament in great numbers, but the northerners were waiting for them and ambushed them, killing many. Then some of the northern lords invaded Scotland and pillaged[3] the county of Carrick.*

Henry Knighton, c. 1400

3. **pillaged:** see page 15.

Various kings struggled for two hundred years to bring Wales under English rule. Edward I (king 1272-1307) finally succeeded and proclaimed his own son Prince of Wales in 1301. The Welsh didn't give up without a struggle, as described by Matthew Paris in his *Historia Anglorum*.

*The Welsh, learning that the king intended to take the field against them with his army, wisely sent away their wives and children, and their flocks, into the interior of the country, round about Snowdon and other mountainous places inaccessible to the English. Then they ploughed up their fields, destroyed the mills along the route the English would take, carried away all kinds of provisions, broke down the bridges, and rendered all the fords impassable by digging holes, so that if the enemy tried to cross, they would be drowned.*

Matthew Paris, c. 1290

## Lawlessness

An English law of 1285 saying that every man must keep arms – 'to keep the peace' – shows that violence was close to everyday life.

*Every man must keep in his house equipment for keeping the peace, according to the old law. That is to say, every man between 15 and 60 years of age must be assessed, and obliged to keep arms according to the amount of land and goods he has. For instance, someone who holds land valued at £15 a year, and goods worth 40 marks[1], must possess a coat of mail, an iron helmet, a sword, a knife, and a horse.*

Statute of Winchester, Chap VI, 1285

1. **mark**: a coin worth 13s (shillings) 4d (old pence) = approx. 66p.

In the countryside, lawless barons and others could make war on both the king and ordinary people. This comes from the forest court rolls of Feckenham in 1280.

*The foresters state that in the forest there is a lawless band of men which varies in number from 15 to 100. They have put themselves under the leadership of Geoffrey of the Park, and a runaway priest or friar whose name is not known. Their stronghold stands at the Gannow in Inkberrow. They have plundered and burned the nighbouring villages, robbing rich and poor alike. They kill the king's deer and the villagers' cattle. At Fepston they burned down a house to create a distraction, while they looted the other houses of the villagers who were putting out the fire. No man is safe from them. They have murdered the king's foresters and terrified the local courts and officials. They have bought and bribed, with stolen money, all the people whom they have not frightened and intimidated.*

Court roll[2], Feckenham, 1280

2. **court roll**: the record of a court's decisions, called a roll because the parchment it was written on was rolled up.

Violence could also be directed at foreigners. Here Richard of Devizes gloats over the murder of Jews at the time of Richard I's coronation in 1189. A hundred years later, all Jews were expelled. Jews were the only people who were allowed to lend money at interest which made them the focus of hatred through much of the medieval period.

*On the day of the coronation, about the time when in the Mass the Son is sacrificed to the Father[3], the Jews in the city of London began to be sacrificed to their father, the Devil... Other towns followed the London faithful, and with the same kind of devotion to religion sent those suckers of blood on their bloody way to hell.*

Richard of Devizes, c. 1200

3. **'Son sacrificed to the Father'**: when mass (the ritual sharing of bread and wine) was given in the church service.

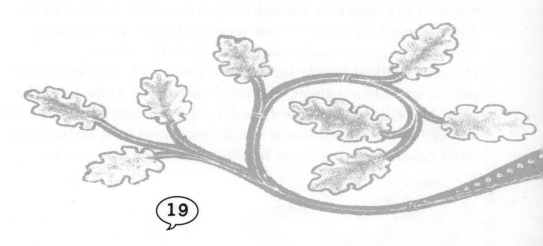

19

# Land, Lord and Peasant

The ideal modern society asks for everyone to be treated equally. They did not think that way in medieval times. Then, society was arranged in levels. One 14th-century preacher said, 'The order of these various ranks in the community ought to be like the position of strings upon the harp ... if the strings are disarranged the melody jars.'

You could also compare it to a pyramid. At the bottom were peasants or villeins[1], freemen[2], servants, and small wage-earners in towns. Above them came knights and squires[3]. Above them came barons, other noblemen and churchmen, some with many estates and farms. Finally, at the very top came the king who owned all land. Everyone else only held it as tenants – from the Latin *tenere*, to hold.

1. & 2. **villeins & freeman:** see page 11.
3. **squire:** a knight's apprentice.

## The Land

Most people worked on the land at this time. Peasants were small-time farmers, working the land in return for services to their lord – usually carting or helping with the harvest. Most of these people were tied to the land of their lord for their lives. The lord also employed farm labourers who would perform work in return for wages, housing and food.

Ploughing the land was hard, as the poet William Langland wrote in his great poem, *The Vision of Piers Plowman*.
*His hood was full of holes and his hair stuck out of it. As he walked his toes peered out from his worn shoes... He was all be-daubed with mud as he followed the plough. He had two thin mittens with worn-out fingers that were thick with muck. This man was almost up to his ankles in mud as he drove along four heifers[4] that were so feeble, such a sorry-looking sight, you could count every rib they had.*
*His wife walked beside him with a long stick in a short coat with a winnowing sheet[5] wrapped round her to keep off the cold. She went barefoot on the ice so the blood flowed. At the end of the row there was a small bowl, and in it lay a small child covered in rags, and two two-year olds were on the*

4. **heifers:** young cows.
5. **winnowing sheet:** a sheet used to winnow wheat (to separate grain from the stalks and husks).

*other side ... and they all cried the same cry till it was sad to hear. The poor man sighed, and said, "Children, be quiet."*

William Langland, c. 1370

In his book about farming, Walter of Henley, tells ploughmen to be cheerful.

*Ploughmen ought not to be gloomy or irritable, but sing and be cheerful, and encourage the oxen in front of them with their songs. They need to take the cattle their straw and their feed, and to be fond of them, and stay with them in the stable at night. They need to make a fuss of them and curry[6] them and rub them down.*

Walter of Henley, 13th century

6. **curry**: brush or groom.

## Feudal Services

In return for land and various rights, tenants paid rent or gave work and services. For perhaps a virgate[7] of land, the small farmer had to work his lord's land for an agreed number of days, and pay for rights – a basket of eggs for the right to keep hens, and so on. Custom decided what these arrangements were, and they varied greatly. Some were harsh, others less so. In time, many services that involved a number of days work were replaced by money payments.

7. **virgate**: a measurement of land – c. 12-15 acres.

Richard le Soper of Pevensey held land from Lewes Priory in Sussex in the 13th century, in return for a rent of 8 shillings[8] a year – and these services:

8. **shilling**: 1s = 5p; 20s = £1.
9. **Lent**: see page 14.

*He [Richard] has to find a man with a wagon and two horses and a cart to cart the lord's dung for one day every year. He must bring half a plough-team to plough at the Lent[9] [spring-time] sowing, and also one other day, and he must bring a horse for one day at each of those times. He must bring a hen at Christmas, and make one journey by pack-horse in Lent from Langrey to Lewes Priory. And he must do one job of carting in summer to bring wood, using a man with two oxen and a wagon with horses, as well as a cart.*

Lewes Priory record, c. 13th century

Sir Peter Miles had very light duties to perform for the Abbess of Caen, who held land round Gloucester.

*Sir Peter Miles, knight, holds from the Lady two virgates[1] of land as well as his great barn, his house and his Hall... In return for all this he promises to come to her court three times a year and to provide his own carts to carry her wool when her Steward sends it to market. Whenever she travels to Gloucester, he will ride along with her, with six of his men. At mowing time he will come himself and lead his servants in the mowing. For other work he does not need to come himself, but must send his men. For rent he promises to pay one red rose at Midsummer.*

Caen Abbey record, late 13th century

After a peasant's death, the lord had the right to reclaim some goods or possessions. Some lords, like the Monks of Vale Royal Manor, were extremely greedy.

*When any peasant who is bound to his lord dies, the lord will take all the pigs of the deceased man, all his goats, all the mares he has in the field, his riding horse, and all his bees. He will take all his pigs for bacon, all his woollen and flaxen cloth, and any gold and silver than can be found. The lord will also have all his brass pots, because he ought to have everything of metal.*

Vale Royal Manor record, 14th century

Peasants who broke rules or did not perform their duties properly could be fined in the lord's manor court. These offences took place 20 years or so before the Black Death of 1348, and 50 or so before the Peasants' Revolt.

*Nine boys and two women were fined 2d[2] and 3d for gleaning[3] badly. Ten of the tenants were fined 2d because they made their sheaves too small – with twisted bands – when they ought to have made sheaves of the same size as those they made when working for the Lady.*

Court roll, c. 1330

1. **virgate**: see page 21.

2. **1d**=2.4p and 240d=100p (£1).
3. **gleaning**: gathering ears of corn left by the reapers in the harvest field.

## Weakening Feudal Ties

Later on, peasants sometimes refused to fulfil their obligations, or just ran away. They also became more independent – especially after the Black Death, when labourers were hard to find. Here some Lincolnshire peasants decide to withhold services.

4. **reeve**: a foreman or farm manager.

*All the tenants holding half a virgate of land, except John Golde, who was the reeve[4] at the time, are fined because they refused to do the carting when summoned.*

*Roger Capon is fined because he refused to come to the barley when he was ordered.*

*Hugh Reeve, Sabina Alwyne, Robert Knyt are fined 6d because they did not come to work when summoned by the reeve.*

Court roll, early 14th century

Throughout this era, certain individuals were freed by their lord, in recognition of good service, or to enter the Church. But by the 15th century, some lords were setting all their peasants free. Here, Edmund, Bishop of Hereford, gives a religious reason why.

5. **piety**: religious duty and belief.

*In the beginning nature created all men free. It was only later that the laws of various nations put the yoke of slavery on the shoulders of some of the people. So I believe that it is an act of piety[5] which will truly deserve a reward from God, to give back their original freedom to those whose qualities demand it.*

Edmund, Bishop of Hereford, 1419

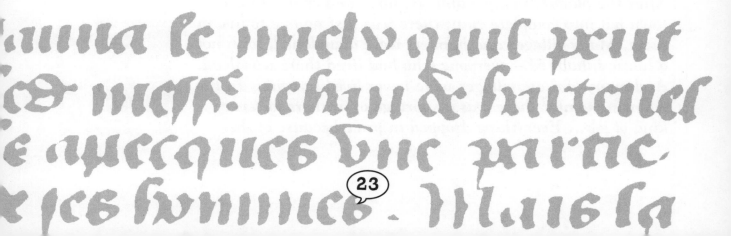

23

# The Black Death and the Peasants' Revolt

These two famous events in the late 14th century changed medieval life for ever. The terrible plague[1], called the Black Death, arrived at Southampton in 1348. It spread through the fleas of black rats jumping ship and raged through England, killing at least a third of the whole population. In London alone, 17,000 people died of it. No one knew how it spread, or how to treat it.

   With so many dead, society began to change. Labourers were in short supply and so could demand higher wages, and their freedom. Discontent was simmering. In 1381, the Peasants' Revolt boiled over, probably due to attempts to collect a tax called a 'poll tax' which some peasants claimed they had already paid.

## The Black Death, 1348

The chronicler[2] Henry Knighton described the arrival of the Black Death.

*This terrible plague travelled inland from Southampton and reached Bristol, where almost the whole population died, as if suddenly struck down. Very few people lingered alive in their beds for more than two or three days, or even half a day. Then this cruel death spread everywhere, following the course of sun [northward]. In the small parish[3] of St Leonard in Leicester three hundred and eighty people died. In the parish of Holy Cross in the same city, four hundred, and in St Margaret's, seven hundred...*
*After the plague, many buildings, large and small, in every town fell into complete ruin; there was just no-one to live in them. Many villages and hamlets were abandoned, with not a house inhabited – everyone who had lived there was dead. And many of these villages were never lived in again. In the following winter there was a shortage of workers for every kind of job... Everything dropped in price because of the*

1. **plague**: a disease transmitted by rat-fleas from rats to people, causing high fever and buboes (swellings of the lymphatic glands).

2. **chronicler**: see page 6.
3. **parish**: area for which each church was responsible.

*general terror of death. Very few people took care of their property and possessions… Many crops rotted in the fields because there was no-one to harvest them.*

Henry Knighton, 1348

A Welsh poet (we don't know his name) wrote these frightening words about the spread of the Black Death:
*We see death coming to us like black smoke, in a plague which kills off the young, a wandering restless being who shows no mercy to a pretty face… The terror of the shilling shape in the armpit … the shape of an apple, with a crown like an onion, the small boil that leaves no-one alone. It scalds, it burns like a cinder.*

Anon, 1348

## The Peasants' Revolt, 1381

People began to question the old order where a relatively small group of people, including the king and barons, lived a life of luxury whilst the peasants worked hard for little gain. The travelling preacher, John Ball, stirred up many peasants with his powerful sermons.

In his *Chronicle of England*, Thomas Walsingham reported John Ball's revolutionary views.
*He taught the people that tithes[4] ought not to be paid unless the person giving them had more wealth than the vicar or rector receiving them. He also taught that tithes should be witheld if the parishioner was a better person than the priest … After being banned by the bishops from preaching in churches he started to preach in the street, in towns and villages, and even in the fields.*

Thomas Walsingham, c. 1388

4. **tithes**: a kind of Church tax, where a tenth of everyone's income was paid to the parish priest.

When Parliament ordered more taxes to be raised to pay for continuing wars in France and Scotland, many peasants were outraged at being asked to pay a tax they felt they'd already paid. The *Anonimalle Chronicle* describes how the King's Council asked Thomas Bampton, a landowner, to collect these taxes.

*Bampton summoned a hundred people from villages and towns locally and told them he needed a new subsidy[1] for the king, ordering them to inquire into the matter, and respond, by paying what they owed. The people from Fobbing replied that they would not pay a penny more because they already had a receipt from him for the subsidy. Thomas Bampton began to threaten them; he had two of the king's sergeants-at-arms with him. The Fobbing people, fearing his anger, decided to discuss the situation with the people of Corringham. The result was that the two townships began to get ... assemblies together, and sent messages to the men of Stanford-le-Hope to suggest they should join in. Then men from all three townships went to Thomas Bampton and told him plainly they would have nothing to do with him or offer him a single penny. Thomas ordered the sergeants to arrest the men and put them in prison. The men resisted and refused to be taken; they tried to kill Thomas and the sergeants. Thomas fled towards London and the council. The people fled into the woods and stayed there a long time, till they were almost dead of hunger. Then they went from place to place stirring up other people to rise against the lords and the good men of the countryside...*

Later...

*Afterwards 50,000 of the common people assembled before Whitsunday and went to the manors and houses of those who did not want to join in the uprising with them, and set fire to their houses or razed them to the ground. At this time they also captured three of Thomas Bampton's clerks and cut off their heads, which they carried round to show others what they could do; it was their idea to kill all the lawyers*

1. subsidy: grant of money.

*and servants of the king that they could find. Meanwhile all the great lords and other people of importance fled to London or into other counties where they could feel safe.*

Anonimalle Chronicle, c. 1381

The uprising grew into a full-scale revolt, led by Wat Tyler and John Ball. In June 1381, Richard II rode out of London to meet the rebels, spoke to Wat Tyler and agreed to his demands. During the peace talks, Wat Tyler was killed and then the rebellion died down fairly quickly. The King did not keep his promises to Tyler, although the unpopular poll tax was abandoned.

The Revolt had sparked off many local uprisings around the country. These too were repressed in the course of year and their leaders executed. Walsingham tells how one rebel leader in St Albans, William Grindcobbe, encouraged his followers to continue the struggle while he was on bail, awaiting trial:

2. **martyr**: one who dies for their beliefs.

*Fellow citizens, for whom a little freedom has now relieved the long years of oppression, stand firm while you can and do not be afraid because I am being persecuted. For if it should happen that I die for the cause of seeking to gain liberty, I will count myself happy to end my life as such a martyr[2]. Act therefore now as you would have acted if I had been beheaded at Hertford yesterday. For nothing could have saved my life if the abbot had not call back his officers in time. They had accused me of many things and had a judge on their side who was eager to shed my blood.*

Thomas Walsingham, c. 1388

Grindcobbe was later executed along with fourteen other St Albans' rebels.

# Food

As a medieval person, what you ate depended on who you were. Lords certainly ate well, with many descriptions of rich feasts running to many courses. Townspeople could eat at home or buy pies and other dishes from pie shops or cook shops. Peasants, if they had enough to eat, probably ate more healthily than their lords in modern terms, using more vegetables and bread in their diet, with some pig meat, cheese and eggs. People ate whatever they could get that was edible, including small birds like thrushes and finches.

## Quantity

Famine was a regular threat in medieval times. As people depended largely on locally-produced food, a disease of people, livestock or crops devasted the food supply.

*Such disease swept through the people that perhaps one person in two was in dire straits from the fever's attack, so that many died. Then, because of the bad weather, a famine throughout England took off many hundreds of people who died of hunger.*

Anglo-Saxon Chronicle, 1087

Three hundred years later, according to the poet William Langland, hunger was still the lot of many poor country labourers 'with many to feed and few pence to do it'.

*Cold flesh and cold fish, instead of roast venison;*
*And on Fridays and feast-days a farthing's worth of mussels*
*Would be a feast day for such folk, or else a few cockles.*

William Langland, c. 1370

Twelfth-century monks fed very well, as Gerald of Wales, Archdeacon of Brecknock, noticed in Canterbury.

*Sitting in the hall with the Prior and the greater monks at the big table, I observed two things ... the excessive amount of gesturing [the monks were forbidden to speak to each other] and the excessive number of dishes... I often heard*

the Prior say that six or more courses were laid in order – or disorder – on the table. And they were sumptuous dishes. At the end ... masses of vegetables and herbs were brought to the table as a separate course, but they were hardly touched, what with so many fishes, roast, boiled, stuffed, fried; so many dishes garnished by the cook's art with eggs and pepper; so many sauces and savouries to rouse gluttonous feelings and excite the appetite.

Gerald of Wales, late 12th century

## Quality

The royal households had a reputation for eating well. Feasts lasted hours and contained many elaborate dishes, including roasted swan. However, in this letter, Peter of Blois, a Frenchman, expresses strong views about food at Court:

I have sometimes seen wine put before noblemen that is so full of dregs that they couldn't drink it properly, and had to filter it through their teeth, keeping their eyes closed. Meat, because it is in great demand, is sold whether or not it's fresh. The fish you buy is four days old, but the fact that it's stinking doesn't affect the price. Servants don't care whether the unlucky guests get ill or die provided they can load their master's table with dishes. In fact the tables are sometimes filled with food that's already gone off badly.

Peter of Blois, 1160

Town and city folk probably experienced the greatest range of food as they could buy from any number of food stalls, cookshops and pastry shops. A good range of food was on offer at this shop in London at regulated prices, as shown in this list taken from an ordinance in 1378.

Best roast pig   8d[1]
Best roast lamb   7d
Best roast goose   7d
Best roast hen   4d

1. 2.4d=1p
12d=1 shilling=5p

29

*Best roast rabbit   4d*
*Best roast river mallard[1]   4¹/₂d*
*Best roast dunghill mallard   3¹/₂d*
*Best roast snipe   1¹/₂d*
*Best roast larks   1¹/₂d*
*Best roast partridge   3¹/₂d*
*Best roast pheasant   13d*
*Best roast curlew   6¹/₂d*
*Three roast thrushes   2d*
*Ten roast finches   2d*
*Best roast heron   18d*
*Best roast bittern   20d*
*For the paste, fire, and trouble upon a goose   2d*
*Ten eggs   1d*

List from London ordinance, 1378

1. **mallard**: type of duck.

In a time before refrigerators and freezers, a lot of food must have gone off although salt was used in abundance to preserve food for the winter. Towns and manors had food regulations — about the correct strength of ale, for instance.

*Assize[2] of Beer: These have all brewed ale which was too weak: Alice, wife of Geoffrey Pigge (fined 1d); Emma, wife of John in the Wood (fined 1d); Blind Kate (fined 1d); Alice, daughter of Thomas Mouse (fined 1d) and Elizabeth, wife of William Ploughman (fined 1d).*

Court roll, 14th century

2. **assize**: a law setting the weight, measurement or price of something.
3. **pillory**: a wooden frame in which a person's head and hands could be locked for a punishment.

Selling unhealthy food was an offence and the punishment could be unpleasant!

*Robert Boucher is fined for selling measled meat, torn and spoiled by dogs. He shall wear it for three days in the pillory[3], stinking round his neck, and in church before services for the next three days.*

Court roll, 14th century

# Trade and Crafts

The wool trade was the 'flower and strength and blood of England', one writer said. By 1300, England had more than 15 million sheep to supply wool for this trade. Certain towns were famous for producing cloth of a particular kind, much of which was exported for profit. Perhaps more than four million people grew rich from this one trade.

There were no factories at this time. Craftsmen in their own workshops made goods, often with the help of apprentices who came to live with them to learn a trade.

Crafts and trades belonged to the countryside as much as to the town. The countryside needed smiths, quarrymen, ropers, plasterers, sawyers, coopers, carters, thatchers, masons, carpenters and more. The city needed gold-workers, shoe-makers, hatters, glass-blowers and builders. Many of the most beautiful buildings standing today were built by medieval craftsmen, such as Durham Cathedral and Lavenham Guildhall.

## The Wool Trade

Raw wool, to make into cloth, was probably the most important English export. In 1337 merchants for William de Pole, taking a consignment of 205 sacks to Flemish clothmakers in Bruges, Ypres and Ghent, charged 18 times what it cost them to buy it, because of all the costs incurred on the 225 day journey from Lincolnshire to Flanders. The 'total cost', recorded in William de Pole's accounts, is before any profit is added.

4. **£, s, d**: see pages 21 and 29.

*Cost of 205 sacks of wool bought in parts in Lindsey £40 0s 10d[4]*
*at 3s 10d per sack*

*Cartage, packing, storage, drying, re-packing, wrapping materials, porterage, hoistage, freightage, shipping, pilotage, armed guard and port dues: £1 14s (4$\frac{1}{2}$d per sack)*
*Value of wool lost from damaged sacks 2s (4$\frac{3}{4}$d per sack)*
*For the expenses of 5 merchants, from September to May 1s (8$\frac{1}{2}$d) per sack*

*Paid to the collectors of royal customs at Hull £1 (6s 8d per sack)*

*Total cost per sack*        *£3 11s ¹⁄4d*
*Total cost of 205 sacks*    *£737 15s 8³⁄4d*

Accounts of William de Pole, 1337

Cloth was made in England too. Chaucer's Wife of Bath has a prosperous cloth-making business. She wears her own expensive 'kerchiefs' at church.

**Of clooth-making she hadde swich an haunt,**
In making cloth she had such a good business,
**She passed hem of Ypres and of Gaunt.**
She surpassed those (manufacturers) of Ypres and Ghent.
**Hir coverchiefs ful fine weren of ground**
Her head-coverings were of very fine texture
**I dorste swere they weyeden ten pound**
I dare swear they weighed ten pound
**That on a Sunday she hadde upon hir heed.**
That on Sundays she wore on her head.

Geoffrey Chaucer, c. 1380

## Craftsmen and Guilds

There would be blacksmiths in most villages. The poet William Langland pictures them at work.

**Swarte-smeked smethes, smatered with smoke,**
Smoke-black smiths, smeared with smoke,
**Drive me to death with den of here dintes:**
Drive me to death with the din of their clanging:
**Swich noise on nights ne herd men never,**
Such noise in the night no-one ever heard,
**What knavene cry and clatering of knockes!**
What workmen's shouts and clattering of blows!
**They blowen their bellewes that all here brain brestes.**
They blow their bellows till their brains are fit to burst.

32

*"Huf, puf," seith that one, "Haf, paf," that other.*
"Huf, puf," says one, "Haf, paf," the other.
*They spitten and sprawlen and spellen many spelles,*
They spit and sprawl and tell many a tale,
*They gnawen and gnacchen, they grones togidre...*
They gnaw and gnash, they groan together...
*Stark strokes they striken on a steled stocke.*
Strong blows they strike on a steel anvil.

William Langland, c. 1370

The craftsmen of London had a reputation for making beautiful objects in precious metal. These instructions come from a book by Alexander of Neckham.
*The goldsmith should have a furnace with a hole at the top so that smoke can get out. One hand should operate the bellows with a light pressure very steadily, so that the air being forced through the tubes heats up the charcoal, and so that the even spread of air heats up the whole fire. There must be an extremely hard anvil on which iron and gold may be softened to take the right shape; then they can be stretched and pulled with the tongs and the hammer. There should be another hammer for making gold leaf, as well as sheets of silver, tin, brass, iron or copper. The goldsmith needs a very sharp chisel with which he can engrave amber, marble, diamond, sapphire or pearl, and make figures in them...*

Alexander of Neckham, 12th century

In order to learn a craft, boys became apprenticed to a craftsman. They usually had a written agreement.
*John Goffe has become apprentice to John Gibbs for eight years. John Gibbs and his wife Agnes shall teach him and train him in the craft of fishing the best way they know how, chastising[1] him when he needs it and providing him with food, clothes and shoes. At the end of eight years, John Gibbs amd his wife shall give John Goffe 20 shillings.*

Indentary agreement, 15th century

1. chastising: beating as a punishment.

33

Craftsmen increasingly had guilds, which made rules for a craft to uphold good standards of work, and ensure the rules were obeyed. Anything not made to standard would be destroyed. Here, the hatters' guild discover 'false hats':

*At the request of the hatters, and the merchants in London who bought and sold hats, it was ordered that immediately after Easter, three or four hatters and hat-merchants should make a search through the city for false hats, and bring any they might find to the Guildhall to be laid before the mayor and aldermen... When the searchers had gone through the city and done their work, they brought to the Guildhall ... certain hats, black, grey and white, which they had found at various haberdashers and hatters. The hats were examined ... and it was found that 40 grey and white hats, and 15 black hats, were of false workmanship, and made of wool and flock. It was therefore decided they should be burnt in the street of Chepe...*

London hustings court, 1311

The 12th-century Abbot of Bury St Edmunds took action against a market set up without his consent – against the law as he saw it.

*The Abbot ordered his bailiffs to gather together the men of St Edmund's, with their horses and arms, and destroy the market, and to tie up and bring back with them the people found buying and selling there. And so in the middle of the night nearly 600 well-armed men set off for Lakenheath. But look-outs gave warning of their coming so that everyone in the market scattered and disappeared, no one was to be found. At the same time, the Prior of Ely came with his bailiffs to protect the buyers and sellers as best he could... When our bailiffs had taken advice about the situation, they pulled to the ground all the stalls and tables of the meat-market, and carried them away, and herded away all the cattle and sheep and oxen.*

Jocelin, c. 1210

# Money and Prices

After the Black Death, skilled labourers were in short supply and increasingly they were freemen[1], not tied to an estate any longer. One unknown writer complained about builders taking it easy.

*They waste a large part of the day, coming to work late, knocking off early, spending a long time over their breakfast ... and taking a lengthy nap in the afternoon.*

Anon, c. 1360

More work was paid for in cash wages after the Black Death, not feudal services.

*Wage of 1 reaper and binder for all autumn   9s[2]*
*For the smith's wages for maintaining the iron parts of ploughs this year   20s besides 3 bushels[3] of wheat*
*For 3 men hired for 1 day to wash and hang herrings   13½d*
*For the wage of one carpenter mending the door, mending the cart and helping make the kiln for 3 days   15d*
*For weeding the lord's corn this year   18d*

Baliff's Account for the Abbot of Dereham, 1366

Some idea of what such wages could buy can be gained from prices paid on the same estate that same year, 1366.

*1 new plough bought   13d[2]*
*12 scythes   4s 4d*
*50 keys   3d*
*1 cow   10s 6d*
*50 sheaves of thatch for roofing   12d*
*Fish: 15 small cods and 20 eels in 1½ gallons[4] of butter 21d*
*1480 herrings   7s*
*7 lb of candles   17½d.*

Baliff's Account for the Abbot of Dereham, 1366

# The Church and Faith

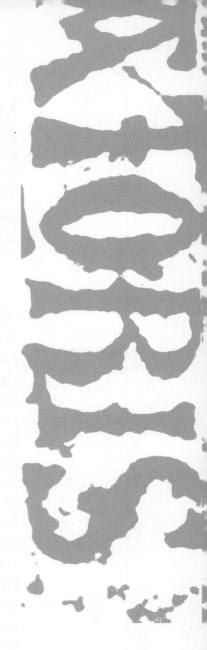

The medieval period was a time of religious belief and great faith. The Church was at the centre of this world, controlling thinking and making rules about conduct. It had its own courts to punish bad behaviour or people who threatened the teachings of the Church. The Church did not look to the king as its ruler but the Pope in Rome.

The Church was one of the great powers of the land, and 'lord' to many people, on innumerable farms where tenants held land in return for rent and services. In 1066, there were approximately 1,000 monks and nuns living a life of prayer and hard work but by 1300 this had grown to about 18,000. Thousands of other people were employed by the Church to look after its lands and possessions. The influence was far-reaching and brought it into conflict with other great powers, such as towns, barons and, of course, the king.

## The Faith

Most medieval people simply believed totally in the Christian faith, following its teachings 'religiously'. For them, there was no doubt that Christ was the son of a Virgin, Mary; that he was crucified and came to life again three days later. As for the horrors of hell – people were terrified by the images of hell drawn by artists and writers, and believed that this would be their fate if they didn't follow the teachings of the Church.

This song to the Virgin Mary, written in the 15th century, gives us a moving picture of medieval faith.

*I sing of a maiden[1]*
*That is makeles[2];*
*King of alle kinges*
*To her sone she ches[3].*

*He cam also stille[4]*
*Ther his moder was*
*As dew in Aprille*
*That falleth on the grass.*

1. **maiden**: virgin.
2. **makeles**: matchless; without equal.
3. **ches**: chose.

4. **also stille**: as quietly

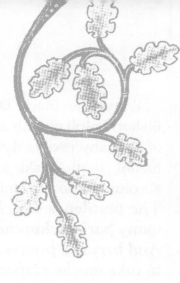

*He cam also stille*
*Ther his moder lay*
*As dew in Aprille*
*That falleth on the spray⁵.*

5. **spray**: a shoot or twig.

*Moder and maiden*
*Was never non but she:*
*Well⁶ may swich a lady*
*Godes moder be.*

6. **Well**: rightly.

Anon, 15th century

Whilst religion was a central part of normal life for everyone, some people, especially if they were wealthy, could organize their whole lives around their faith. This is the daily religious routine of Cecily, Duchess of York, the mother of Edward IV. The book — written in English by Cecily — also describes other rules for her household.

*She usually gets up at seven, and her chaplain is waiting to say the matins⁷ of the day and of our Lady with her. When she is ready she hears a low mass in her room and after that has some breakfast. She goes to the chapel to hear the divine service and two low masses, and from there she goes to dinner. During dinner she hears a reading on a holy topic... After dinner she has meetings for an hour with anyone who needs to see her, then she sleeps for a quarter of an hour. After her rest she spends the time in prayer until the first bell rings for evensong. Then she enjoys a drink of wine or ale... After the last bell has rung she goes to the chapel and hears evensong. From there she goes to supper where she reads the passage she heard at dinner to those who are with her. After supper she spends time with her gentlewomen enjoying some innocent diversion and relaxation. An hour before bed she has a cup of wine, then she goes to her private room and takes leave of God for the night.*

7. **matins**: morning prayers.

Cecily, Duchess of York, c. 1480

When the Black Death killed many priests in 1348-9, Bishop Ralph of Bath and Wells was very worried by the idea of so many people dying without a visit from a priest. This meant they could not confess their sins and receive absolution[1], so preventing them from entering heaven.

*The pestilence which is now spreading everywhere has left many parish churches and other places without a priest... And because priests cannot be found, not for love or money, to take on the responsibility for those places and visit people who are ill and administer the sacraments[2] to them – perhaps because priests are frightened of catching the plague themselves – many are dying without the sacrament of penance[3].*

Bishop Ralph of Bath and Wells, January 1349

1. **absolution:** formal forgiveness of sins by a priest.
2. **sacrament:** a special religious ceremony or rite conducted by a priest.
3. **penance:** see page 14.

## Working for the Church

Joining the Church, with the Lord's permission, was a way of escaping a life tied to the land. Alice Barley from Lincolnshire, wrote a letter on behalf of her son.

*Alice Barley pays the Lady 5 shillings to have her son Peter ordained[4]. Granted by a letter from the Abbess.*

Alice Barley, c. 1320

4. **ordained:** officially made into a priest.

The Church at its best worked hard for people. Chaucer admired the hard-working honesty of a priest.

*Ful looth were hym to cursen for his tythes*
He would never bully or nag to get his tithes[5]
*But rather wolde he yiven, out of doute,*
He'd sooner be making gifts, for sure, without a doubt,
*Unto his povre parishens aboute*
To all his poor parishioners round about
*Of his offryng and eek of his substaunce.*
From the offerings made to him and what he owned.
*He could in litl thyng have suffisaunce.*
He could make do with very little.

5. **tithes:** see page 25.

*Wyd was his parisshe, and houses fer asunder,*
His parish was large, with houses far from each other,
*But he ne lefte nat, fer rain ne thonder,*
But he didn't neglect, come rain or thunder,
*In siknesse nor in meschief to visite*
In illness or misfortune to visit
*The ferreste in his parrishe, muche and lite.*
The furthest away on his parish, great or humble.

Geoffrey Chaucer, c. 1380

But some monks and nuns evidently liked animals more than people! After inspecting a nunnery, Bishop Wykeham made these comments in a letter.

*Some of the nuns of your house bring birds, rabbits, dogs and such-like into the Church, and pay more attention to them than to church services... As a result of hunting hounds and dogs living within the precincts of the monastery, the alms money set aside for the poor is eaten up in food for them, and the church buildings and the cloister are fouled and dirty. Also, because of the terrible din they make, divine services are frequently interrupted. So we strictly command you, Lady Abbess, to have these dogs removed.*

Bishop Wykeham, 1387

## The Church and Its Funding

Many people thought the Church was corrupt, making money improperly, stealing from the poor and breaking their vows of faith. The Church sometimes looked greedy and uncaring. In Jocelin of Brakelond's chronicle of the life of the Abbey of Bury St Edmunds in Suffolk he describes how Abbot Samson changed the customary way the Abbey collected 'repsilver' – a penny each household paid the Abbey to avoid having to go and cut its corn.

*The abbot thought that the way the cellarer[6] went round*

6. **cellarer**: a monastery official responsible for food supplies and trade with the world outside.

39

*the town collecting 'repsilver' was undignified. When poor people couldn't pay the cellarer would take away some of their belongings as security – stools, doors, other essential things. Little old women came out of their houses angrily brandishing distaffs[1], shouting at the cellarer and his officers and threatening them. The abbot decided that 20s should be paid every year at the borough court instead.*

1. **distaff:** stick used to spin by hand.

Jocelin, c. 1210

The Church made money out of people's fear about the after-life. Official Pardoners sold religious relics and other pardons from the Pope, letting people off their penances[2] and so speeding their way out of purgatory[3] and on into heaven. Chaucer gives us a picture of a corrupt Pardoner, who carries false religious relics and 'pardons', deceiving innocent folk.

2. **penance:** see page 14.
3. **purgatory:** a mid-way place between heaven and hell where a person's spirit could go after death.

*In his bag he kept a pillow-case*
*Which, he claimed, was the Virgin Mary's veil.*
*He also swore he had a length of sail*
*From St Peter's boat, when he used to be*
*A fisherman, before Jesus Christ summoned him from*
*  Galilee.*
*And with these 'relics', whenever he found*
*Some poor peasant working on the land,*
*In one day he made himself more profit*
*Than the poor peasant earned in a month and more.*

Geoffrey Chaucer, c. 1380

But the incredible power attributed to a genuine religious relic is shown by this description of what happened after Archbishop Thomas Becket was murdered in 1170. Becket had fallen foul of King Henry II who wanted to claim back some of the power of the Church for himself. When Becket defended the Church's rights, Henry was furious and is said to have ordered some knights to kill Becket. This account of the scene following the murder in Canterbury Cathedral was

written by Benedict, a monk from Peterborough. Once the alarm was given, the townsfolk of Canterbury came pouring into the cathedral.

*While the body still lay on the pavement, some of them [the townsfolk] smeared their eyes with blood. Others brought bottles and carried off secretly as much as they could. Others cut off shreds of clothing and dipped them in the blood. Later on, no-one considered themselves happy unless they had taken away something from the precious treasure of the martyr's[4] body... Some of the blood left over was carefully and cleanly collected and poured into a clean vessel and treasured up in the church.*

Benedict, c. 1190

4. **martyr**: see page 27.
5. **heretic**: see page 4.

## Dissent in the Ranks

Some people came to disbelieve some of the Church's teaching whilst others continued to worship but were critical of the corruption of some churchmen. Margery Baxter was tried for heresy, a serious crime of denying the teachings of the Church. Joan Clyfland, a witness, describes how she was rebuked by Margery for kneeling in church before the cross. Margery might have been burnt as a heretic[5], if she had not been pregnant.

*She [Margery] said, "You do wrong kneeling and praying in front of images in church because God is never present in a church; he has never left heaven, and never will..." And she said, "There is no need to honour images in church any more than there is to bow down in front of the gallows. And if you are keen to see the true cross of Christ, I will show it to you here." And the witness said that she would be glad to see it. And Margery said, "Look," stretching her arms wide, "this is the true cross of Christ, and this is the cross you should worship every day in your own home. You're wasting your time in church worshipping and praying to dead images and crosses."*

Court record, c. 1430

# Crusaders and Pilgrims

The Christian faith was a central part of medieval life yet, leading a religious life and believing in the teachings of the Church was not enough for some people. So they set off on religious Crusades and pilgrimages.

Richard I was more concerned with fighting the Muslims on Crusades in the Holy Land than in governing his own country.

Meanwhile, thousands of pilgrims from all but the poorest backgrounds travelled all over England and Europe to better their chances of entering heaven. Chaucer's famous *Canterbury Tales* describes pilgrims telling stories to pass the time as they journeyed to Canterbury, to worship at the shrine of Archbishop Thomas Becket.

## Crusaders

The Crusades were religious wars fought mostly against the Muslims in the Middle East and North Africa, but also against other Christians in Europe. Guibert of Nogent, a monk, justified Crusades in his *History of the First Crusade*.

***God has instituted holy wars in our time so that the order of knights and the crowd of people following in their wake have a new way of gaining heavenly salvation.***

Guibert of Nogent, c. 1110

Early Crusades were against 'infidel' non-Christians. In 1095, the Pope, head of the Christian Church, called for the holy places of Palestine to be freed from Muslim control. Unfortunately, the Christian Holy Land was also the Islamic Holy Land and neither side was prepared to give it over to the other. Jerusalem, a holy city for both religions, was captured by the Muslims in 1187 and pilgrims were no longer able to travel to the city.

Two hundred years later, an Arab historian, Baha' ad-Din, told how King Richard the 'Lion Heart' of England, wrote to Saladin, leader of the Muslims.

*In 587 [1191] King Richard wrote to the Sultan. "I greet you," he said, "and remind you that Muslims and Franks are bleeding to death. The country is completely ruined, with property and belongings destroyed, and lives sacrificed on both sides. The time has come to stop this. Jerusalem is an object of worship to us... The land from here to beyond the Jordan must be handed over to us. The Cross, which is nothing to you but a worthless piece of wood, is enormously important to us. If the Sultan will return it to us, we can make peace..."*

Saladin wrote back:

*"Jerusalem is as much ours as it is yours. Indeed, it is more sacred to us than to you, for it is the place where our prophet, Muhammed, made his final journey, and where we shall all be gathered on the day of the Last Judgement. This land was always ours, but you have come here only recently, and taken it from us. As for the Cross, it cannot be surrendered except for something equally valuable to Islam."*

Baha' ad-Din, Christian date c. 1200 (Islamic date c. 600)

One of the pilgrims in Chaucer's *Canterbury Tales* is a knight. He crusaded in many places in Northern Africa and Europe. 'His lordes war' was perhaps Henry IV's in Granada, Spain, in 1343. Crusades in southern Spain were against the Jewish and Muslim populations living mainly in Cordoba, Seville and Granada. They were all driven from Spain by the late 15th century.

**At Alisaundre he was when it was wonne.**

He was at Alexandria when it was taken.

**Ful ofte tyme he had the bord bigonne**

Many a time he had sat at the head of the table

**Aboven alle nacions in Pruce.**

Above knights of other countries in Prussia.

**In Lettow had he reysed and in Ruce,**

He had been on military expeditions in Lithuania and Russia,

*No Christen man so ofte of his degree.*
No Christian of his rank so often.
*In Gernade at the seege eek hadde he be*
He had also been in Granada at the siege
*Of Algezir, and riden in Belmarye.*
Of Algezir, and fought in Benmarin [modern Morocco].
*Ay Lyeys was he and at Satalye...*
He was at Lyas [Armenia] and Satalye [Turkey]...

Geoffrey Chaucer, c. 1380

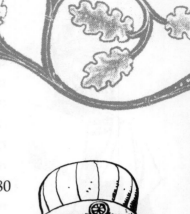

Crusades were also launched against Christian rulers who quarrelled amongst themselves. The chronicler, Henry Knighton, describes how in 1383 the Bishop of Norwich raised money for a Crusade in France.

*The bishop had collected a massive amount ... in gold and silver, jewels, necklaces, rings, plate, carved figures, pearls and other ornaments, especially from women...*
*There was no absolution[1] unless you gave as much as your possessions made it possible for you to.*

Henry Knighton, c. 1400

1. **absolution:** see page 38.

This French Crusade captured Dunkirk in 1383. Its success was inspiring:

*This good news reached England... The truth of what the crusaders said was clear from the war-prizes they brought back with them – stallions, mares, bullocks, and many household furnishings. At once the whole country, tempted by the thought of such booty was roused to set out. In London, many apprentices ... immediately fitted themselves out in white cowls, with red crosses on the right side, and red sheaths for their swords on the left, and set off without even asking the permission of their masters. All over England others did the same, leaving family and friends, armed with nothing but swords, bows and arrows... They brought great dishonour on themselves, because they were not undertaking this great pilgrimage for the sake of Jesus, but to see the country and the world.*

Thomas Walsingham, c. 1388

# Pilgrims

Pilgrimage was a part of the medieval way of life. Pilgrims travelled through England, visiting shrines. Others travelled abroad, particularly to Jerusalem (when they could), Rome and Spain. They might be forgiven their sins if they prayed at the tomb of a saint, helping their passage into heaven.

Chaucer's Wife of Bath is a great traveller on pilgrimages.
*And thries hadde she been at Jerusalem;*
*She hadde passed many a straunge strem[2];*
*At Rome hadde she been, and at Boloigne,*
*In Galice at Seint-Jame[3], and at Coloigne.*

Geoffrey Chaucer, c. 1380

2. **straunge strem:** foreign river.
3. **In Galice at Seint-Jame:** In Galicia at St James' [of Compostela, a shrine]

Pilgrimages must have been fun in some ways, travelling in a group and seeing new places. But people like William Thorpe, giving evidence in a church court, disapproved.
*And in every town they go through, what with the noise of their singing and their bagpipes, the jangling of their bells and the dogs barking after them, they make more din than if the King came by with all his trumpets sounding out and all his minstrels.*

Court records, 1407

Travel in medieval times could be risky, what with leaky ships, filthy hostels and highwaymen. The sheer endurance needed on some journeys added to the spiritual gain of the pilgrimage. Brother John of Canterbury has difficulty writing on his pilgrimage, as related in this letter.
*Forgive me for not writing. I have been on the Mountain of Jupiter [Great St Bernard]... I reached my hand into my bag to scratch down a few words to you – I found my ink-bottle filled with a mass of ice. My fingers refused to write. My beard was stiff with frost, and my breath congealed in a long icicle.*

Brother John of Canterbury, 1188

# Man and Wife

The Church took control over marriage during William the Conqueror's reign when it was decreed that all marriages needed the approval of the Church. The Church said girls had to be 12 to marry and boys 14, although they could be engaged at 7. In practice, few people married as early as this, especially the peasant class.

Many people entered into marriage more as a practical arrangement rather than in a spirit of love. The well-off people have left us letters and other writings that show us some thoughts on medieval marriage and family life.

The poorer people did not write about their lives as the rich did. We hear more about them – in manor records for instance – than direct from them.

## Marriage

At the Council of Winchester in 1076 the Church took control over marriage.

*No-one should give his daughter or any other relative to anyone without the blessing of a priest, otherwise it will not be a proper marriage.*

Records from the Council of Winchester, 1076

With the Church's permission, royal princes and princesses could marry very young.

*The marriage of the King of England's son and the King of France's daughter was celebrated ... the boy was only five years old and the girl, three.*

Chronicle kept by the monks of Bury St Edmunds, 1160

Church control over marriage was confirmed a few years later. Some of the rules established at this time stay true to this day. Now the bans[1] are read three times before a marriage date to ensure that the public have a chance to inform the priest of any reason why the couple should not marry.

*No-one may be joined in matrimony except publicly in front of the church and in the presence of a priest...*

1. **bans**: a formal announcement of the marriage between two people.

*No marriage shall be contracted without it being publicly announced three times in church.*

Council of Westminster, 1200

2. **manor**: see page 11.
3. **fee**: land or manor.
4. **mark**: see page 18.

Marriages needed the lord's permission also, especially if they were to be performed outside the manor[2].
*Roger Legat pays 20s for permission to marry his daughter Amita out of the fee[3] of the Lady, namely to John Austin of Harston.*

Court roll, Lincolnshire, early 14th century

Marrying without the permission of the lord or lady was dangerous.
*It is ordered to seize into the Lady's hands a house and land which Matilda Kreyk held, because she has married a certain free man who is not bound to the land of the Lady.*

Court roll, Maddingly, early 14th century

## Arranged Marriages

When wealthy people married, it was partly a business deal, with land and money an important part of the negotiations. This letter from the Paston Letters (1422-1509), shows how the negotiations were progressing for the marriage of this young woman, Margery Drews, to her 'valentine', John Paston III. She begins:

*Right worshipful and well-beloved Valentine,*
*I have to say plainly to you that my father will part with no more money for the marriage than £100 and 50 marks[4], which is a long way short of what you want. So, if you could be content with that, and my poor self, I would be the happiest young woman on earth. If you do not think that amount would satisfy you, or you do want greater wealth, as I have understood from you before, my good, true and loving Valentine, do not trouble to come here again about it, but let it go, and not be talked about again...*

Paston Letters, 1478

47

# A Woman's Lot

Once married, women were expected to obey their husbands in most things. Wealthy medieval women had power over their households, busily organizing a range of workmen and servants for the upkeep of the house, and tutors for their children. Poorer women worked hard all their lives, struggling to keep their children healthy and make their husbands' earnings provide food on the table. Rich or poor, women didn't have the power to change their lives.

Church court records often mention domestic violence.

*Thomas Louchard beat his wife. He appears before the court. He confesses, and is whipped in the usual way, once through the market. He went away.*

Court record, Droitwich, 1300

A church court record from Buckinghamshire shows that wives were sometimes sold.

*Thomas Godyng sold his wife and now has another. He appeared before the court and confessed that he has a wife. He is ordered to leave the other woman alone.*

Church court record, Buckinghamshire, 1486

The lives of poor people were hard. There was much anti-woman feeling, but this ballad about a tyrannical husband shows there was also sympathy for them.

*The peasant and his lad went off to the field to plough.*
*His wife had a lot to do,*
*with a number of small children to look after.*
*and no servant to help her.*

*The peasant came home early,*
*expecting to find everything just as he'd like it.*
*"Wife," he said, "is the dinner ready?"*
*"No," she said,. "How can I do more than I can?"*

*He began to get angry with her. "Damn you!" he said,*
*"You ought to try ploughing with me,*
*Walking all day on wet boggy clods,*
*Then you would know what hard work it is being a*
*ploughman."*
*...*
*So his wife said, "You can rot!*
*I have more to do than you, all things considered.*
*Even when I'm in bed I only get a bit of sleep,*
*But then early in the morning you shout to me to get up.*

*I've lain awake all night with our child,*
*But I get up and find our house in chaos,*
*Then I milk our cows and turn them out in the field,*
*And all the while you're still sound asleep. Christ protect*
*me!"*

Anon, 15th century

Medieval books taught behaviour – for all kinds of people. Here a writer, speaking as a father to his daughters, gives advice on how to be a good wife.

*Therefore the wife ought to allow her husband to be*
*spokesman and master, as that is her duty, and it is*
*shameful to hear strife between them, especially in front of*
*other people. When they are alone, she can talk to him*
*pleasantly, and advise him to mend his ways if he has done*
*wrong... Fair daughters, hold it in your heart not to put any*
*paint or make-up, on your faces which were made in God's*
*image. Keep them as your creator and nature have*
*ordained. Do not pluck your eyebrows or your temples or*
*forehead. Do not wash your hair in anything but soap and*
*water.*

Book of the Knight of La Tour Landry, c. 1372

# Childhood and Education

Until the age of seven or eight most children learned skills at home and played. Girls helped to cook and bake, look after younger children, attend to animals and wash clothes. Boys went out to the fields with their fathers or started to learn their father's trade. A medieval book says: 'A carpenter teaches his son to cut with an axe, the smith his son to work with a hammer.'

The children of the wealthy would receive an education. Tutors were employed to teach them, along with any pages[1] living in the household. From the 12th century there were some schools in towns. Village schools started up, usually run by a priest who taught the Lord's Prayer and the ABC. Most people below the rank of a substantial freeholder would be illiterate, as would their children.

1. **page**: a boy training to be a knight in a noble's household, receiving his education in return for services.

## Brought Up Away from Home

From the start of the medieval period, children from all levels of society were often sent away from home to be educated or given a training. Nobles wanted their children to be pages in other households. There, manners were taught, along with hunting, archery and some education.

Gervase of Tilbury, a member of the household of William archbishop of Rheims, mentions an interesting English custom, and a reason for it.

*It is the custom among the greatest nobles of England to send their sons to be brought up in France in order to be trained in arms and have the barbarity of their native language removed.*

Gervase of Tilbury, late 12th century

Many years later, wealthy English people believed that there were good reasons for sending their children away.

*The sons of the nobles in England cannot easily degenerate but will rather surpass their ancestors in honesty, vigour and fineness of manners – because they will be trained in a*

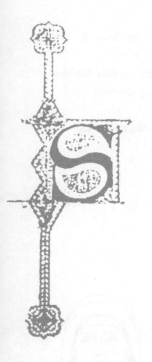

household which is a superior and nobler household to that of their parents.

*Sir John Fortescue, 15th century*

In noble households especially, manners were a crucial part of young people's upbringing. Books of manners were important guides to behaviour. In John Russell's *Book of Nurture*, he gives advice.

*Do not claw your head or your back as if you were after a flea, or stroke your hair as if you were looking for a louse.*
*Do not pick your nose, or let it drip, or sniff, or blow so loud your lord hears it.*
*Do not belch, or spit too far, or laugh or talk too loudly.*
*Beware of making faces and sneering. Don't tell lies with your mouth. And don't lick your lips or dribble.*
*Do not lick a dish with your tongue to get out dust.*
*Eating in company is important.*
*Whether you spit near or far, hold your hand in front of your mouth to hide it.*

*John Russell, c. 1360*

## Schools

William Fitzstephen shows the medieval curriculum in action.

*On feast days the masters assemble in the churches to celebrate. The scholars debate... The boys of different schools have competitions with each other in composing verse, and also in the principles of grammar, such as the rules of the past tense.*

*William Fitzstephen, late 12th century*

School might start as early as six. This fine excuse for being late, due to milking the ducks, receives a harsh response!

*On Monday morning when I shall rise,*
*At six of the clock, it is the gise[2]*
*To go to skole[3] without avise[4] —*

2. **the gise**: the usual thing.
3. **skole**: school.
4. **avise**: a thought.

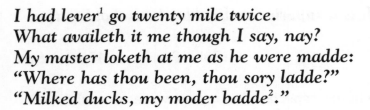

**Childhood and Education**

*I had lever[1] go twenty mile twice.*
*What availeth it me though I say, nay?*
*My master loketh at me as he were madde:*
*"Where has thou been, thou sory ladde?"*
*"Milked ducks, my moder badde[2]."*

*My master peppered my arse with good speed*
*He would not leave till it bleed*
*I would my master were an hare,*
*And all his bokes[3] houndes were –*
*And I myself a joly hunter*
*To blow my horn I would not spare.*

Anon, 15th century

1. **lever**: would sooner.
2. **my moder badde**: as my mother told me to.
3. **bokes**: books.

Beating was a feature of schooling through this time. Agnes Paston asks a messenger to speak to her son's teacher. *Ask him to send word in writing how well Clement Paston has done his duty in learning. And if he has not done well, and will not improve, ask him to belash him well and truly till he does. His last master did, the best he ever had at Cambridge.*

Agnes Paston, c. 1470

By the 15th century there were many grammar schools. Though most were not free, prominent people came through them from poor families. A law of 1406 said that 'any man or woman, of any estate and condition, shall be free to put his son or daughter to learn letters in any school in the kingdom'.

Archbishop Rotherham founded a school at Rotherham, then he appointed a third teacher.

*In the third place, because the county produces many youths gifted with the light and sharpness of ability, who do not all wish to attain the dignity and elevation of the priesthood, so that these youths may be better fitted for mechanical arts and other concerns of this world, we have selected a third*

*teacher learned and skilled in the art of writing and accounts.*

Archbishop of Rotherham, 1483

## Three Languages

French was the official 'English' language for more than two hundred years, and many children learned all their lessons in French until perhaps the late 13th century. At Cambridge and Oxford, where there were perhaps 3,000 students towards the late medieval time, studies were in Latin.

Ranulph Higden, a monk complained about children having to neglect their own language in school.

*Children at school are made to do the opposite of what happens everywhere else in the world, and do all their lessons and everything else speaking French, not using their own native langauge. And that has gone on since the Normans first came to England. The children of nobles are taught to speak in French from when they are babies... And anyone who wants to impress will imitate a gentleman and try to communicate in French.*

Ranulph Higden, 1342

## University

The first university started in Oxford and scholars gathered in a few other towns around England. In the early 13th century, a few Oxford students sought refuge in Cambridge after a scandal which led to the founding of Cambridge University. Only scholars from wealthy families could attend university as it was costly.

These regulations for the students at King's College in the 15th century give a picture of life at Cambridge.

*While they are sat at table in the hall each day, all the students, chaplains and clerics[4] of King's College will have the Bible read to them publicly – or writings of the holy fathers and teachers. They will all listen carefully while*

4. **clerics:** see page 15.

*they eat in silence. No one will interrupt the reading by talking, or telling stories, or making a noise of any kind, or creating a disturbance.*

*None of the students, fellows, chaplains, clerics or servants of King's College are to keep dogs, or nets for hunting, or ferrets, or falcons, or hawks. Nor can they practise hunting or fishing, or possess an ape, bear, fox, stag, hind, doe, badger, or any other wild animal or bird... The fellows and students are forbidden to throw stones, balls, lumps of dirt, spears, or anything else, or play games... which may cause damage to any church, hall, house, or other buildings of the college...*

Cambridge University, 15th century

Richard Aungerville, tutor to Edward III and later Bishop of Durham, writing about the care of books, gives us a vivid picture of a student.

*Because it is winter, and he feels chilly, his nose runs, and he doesn't even bother to wipe it before it starts dripping down on his book. He should really have a shoemaker's apron, not a book. He has long fingernails, black as coal, and marks the passages he likes with them. He puts innumerable straws in different parts of the book, so that their stems will help him to find parts he can't remember. The book can't take all these straws, and gets so thick with them it bursts its clasps... This type of student doesn't think twice about eating his cheese and fruit over an open book, or putting his cup down on this page then that. He has no bag handy either, so he leaves the crumbs and scraps in the book. He carries on chatting with his friends all the time, scattering saliva everywhere. Then, even worse, he puts his head down for a nap and smoothes out the wrinkles on the page by creasing it double.*

Richard Aungerville, 1345

# Health and Medicine

Much of the knowledge about the human body that we take for granted had not been discovered in medieval times. Doctors worked with no real knowledge about the causes of diseases or how they developed or spread.

Many religious houses ran hospitals, caring for the sick without any real hope of curing them. However, during medieval times, serious doctors and medical writers started making discoveries. Great hospitals were founded and laws and regulations showed a desire to improve public health.

## Doctors

Medieval doctors were not well trained, or very skilful. Some did study at university and became learned physicians, but many were barber-surgeons. John of Salisbury, like many others, didn't think much of them.

*They come home from college full of fine theories, keen to practise what they have learned… They have handy sayings for every topic, and they make their listeners gape at their long-winded, high-flown language. Innocent people believe doctors can do anything because that is the impression they create. When I hear them talk, I fancy they can raise the dead… They have only two rules, which they never break – don't bother about the poor, and never refuse money… What shall I say about practising doctors? God forbid I should say anything about them, because I fall into their hands all too often.*

John of Salisbury, 12th century

Much medieval medicine was based on astrology, which they called astronomy. Some doctors used this knowledge to decide when to give a medicine or do an operation.

John of Burgundy, a doctor, writes about the stars in his book, *De Pestilentia Liber*.

*In more than 40 years of practice I have proved that a medicine given in opposition to the signs of the constellations, even though it is skilfully compounded and blended, and put together according to the laws of medicine, will do nothing useful for the patient. Without astronomy medicine is of little use...*

John of Burgundy, 14th century

Throughout this time, barbers might work as surgeons. This barber-surgeon failed to treat the patient.

*Adam Leche, a barber of Spital Street is fined 6s and expelled from the town because he failed to treat Richard Ome's wounded arm, so that it is now to be amputated, with great danger to the said Richard's life. The fine will be paid to Richard's wife for loss of his earnings, as well as a halfpenny a week from the Common Coffer for his children's welfare.*

Court record, c. 1410

John Aderne, a surgeon, gives doctors some tips.

*Make sure that the fee is adjusted to the man's standing in life; never ask too little.*
*If the patients or their friends ask how long it will take for you to heal them, always say about twice as long as it will really take. So if the doctor hopes for a cure in twenty weeks, add the same number on top of that... A young doctor should also learn useful proverbs and tales and sayings relating to his work to cheer his patients up with.*

John Aderne, 14th century

## Cures

Most cures were based on magic or herbal remedies. This is for toothache from a Welsh manuscript.

*Take a candle made from mutton fat, in which is mixed the seed of sea-holly. Let the candle burn as close as possible to the tooth, holding a basin of cold water underneath. The worms which are gnawing the tooth will fall into the water*

56

*to escape the heat of the candle*.

It also suggests a cure for quinsy, a severe throat infection.
*Take a fat cat, skin it, and draw out the guts, then take the grease of a hedgehog and the fat of a bear, and some sage, and gum of honeysuckle... Crumble all this up to a powder and stuff the cat-skin with it. Then roast it, and gather up the grease and oil the patient with it.*

Meddygon Mydveu, 14th century

Perhaps because doctors were little help, medieval people believed in miracle cures. Here the writer describes how a miracle brought the son of Matilda of St Hilary, back to life. Whilst Matilda is at a church, her son dies. She rushes home and the story continues.
*She took him in her arms and said, "St Thomas, give me back my son. When he had a hernia once you saved him. Now he is dead restore him to me, holy martyr[1], restore him to life..." She ran and took from a chest the relics of the saint which she had brought from Canterbury. She put the blood of the saint on the mouth of the dead infant and thrust a piece of cloth into his throat, crying all the time, "Holy St Thomas, give me back my son..." After she had cried like this for about two hours, the martyr had mercy and restored the infant to life...*

Anon, c. 1170-73

1. **martyr:** see page 27.

## Health Laws

As the medieval period moved on, court judgements and regulations show a growing concern about health matters.
*John Knight and Rose his wife are lepers[2] but they come into the market to sell chickens and eggs, so that other may take their sickness. They are to be whipped out of town.*

Court roll, c. 1410

2. **leper:** a person suffering from leprosy, an disfiguring and incurable disease at the time.

# Games and Pastimes

At this time, the main recreation of kings and lords – hunting – was forbidden to the poor. Tournaments were too expensive for most people to attend yet people found ways to amuse themselves, especially on the holy days, or holidays, that occurred throughout the year.

At home there were board- and card-games for long winter evenings and traditional games that children played for fun. There was music – singing together for fun or playing musical instruments. Well-off women did embroidery.

Outdoor pleasures included fishing and poaching. There was something called 'football' and another game called 'tenys'. There were taverns, one or two with names such as le Bull, le Swanne, and le Frogge, to meet with friends.

## Feast Days

William Fitzstephen writing in his *History of Thomas Becket*, gives us a vivid picture of people enjoying themselves on holy days in early medieval London. These days must have been a great release from the drudgery of working lives.

*On feast-days throughout the summer the youths take their exercise with jumping, wrestling, and archery... Each year on the day called Carnival ... schoolboys bring fighting cocks to their master, and the whole morning is spent watching cock-fighting; they have a school holiday to watch them scrap. After dinner all the young folks from the city go out into the fields to play ball games. The pupils from each school have their own ball, and the workers from each trade too. Older men and fathers and rich people come on their horses to watch the young people's games...*

*Nearly every feast-day in winter, before dinner, there are boars foaming with sweat, and pigs with fierce tusks – on the way to being bacon – and big bulls with great horns, and huge bears, fighting to the death against the dogs that are let loose on them.*

*When the great marsh on the north side of the city's north walls is frozen over, crowds of young lads go out on the ice. Some accelerate at a run, then with their feet well apart, glide sidelong over the frozen waste. Others make seats out of blocks of ice like millstones and get dragged along by a chain of others linking hands... Some of them fit animal shin-bones to their feet, tied round at the ankle, and use iron-sheathed poles to propel themselves along, striking the ice and powering along as fast as a bird flying...*

William Fitzstephen, c. 1180

## Processions and Tournaments

1. **pageant**: a street spectacle or performance usually involving some kind of procession; similar to a carnival today.

People loved display, like this pageant[1], described by Thomas Walsingham, monk of St Albans, which was put on by guilds of London craftsmen for Richard II's coronation in 1377.

*The guilds had large groups of flutes and trumpets – every guild is led by its trumpeters. Trumpeters had been stationed at the top of a tower which had been built in the King's honour, to sound a fanfare as he approached... And in the shopping street called Cheapside a kind of castle had been built, with four towers ... where four beautiful women of about the King's age waited, dressed in white... As the King approached, they scattered golden leaves in front of him, and as he got nearer, they showered imitation gold coins over him and his horse. When he reached the front of the castle, they took gold cups and filled them with the wine that spilled from spouts in the castle towers, and offered them to the king. At the very top of the castle stood a golden angel holding a golden crown. She had been positioned so cleverly that when the king arrived, she could bend down to offer him the crown.*

Thomas Walsingham, c. 1390

Jean Froissart saw the jousting[1] tournament which Richard II arranged in London, 'for tilting courteously, with blunted lances' and wrote about it in his Chronicle.

*When Sunday came, about three o'clock, there came pounding from the Town of London ... sixty coursing[2] horses in cloths and coats and ornamented for the tournament, with a squire[3] of honour mounted on each one...*

*When the ladies leading the knights reached the square, servants were waiting to help them dismount and take them to the apartments reserved for them. The knights waited until the squires had dismounted and brought them their coursers. They mounted, had their helmets laced on, and prepared themselves in every way for the tilt[4]. When the tournament began every one exerted himself to the limit. Many were unhorsed, many more lost their helmets...*

*On the Tuesday ... the supper was as before at the Bishop's Palace, and the dancing lasted till daybreak... The rest of the week was spent feasting.*

Jean Froissart, 1390

These ladies at a tournament in 1347 might have been hurt, as Geoffrey le Baker reports in *Chronicon*.

*A little before the feast of St Michael in London at the place called Chepe there were very beautiful lists[5]. But the Lady Queen Philippa and a large party of ladies were thrown to the ground when the pavilion from which they were watching the jousting collapsed. Fortunately they were not hurt, and the Queen would not hear of the carpenters being punished. Indeed she went down on bended knee before the angry king and his retinue, bringing calm with her prayers and pleading.*

Geoffrey le Baker, c. 1350

1. **joust**: a formal fight between two horsemen.

2. **coursing**: hunting.
3. **squire**: see page 20.

4. **tilt**: a horse-back charge or attack using a lance or spear.

5. **lists**: the grounds where a joust took place.

# Outdoor Sport for the Masses

After the Black Death, Edward III was concerned about being able to find enough battle-winning archers. He wrote to sheriffs[6] all round England and in the process tells us about all the other sports that people were doing.

6. **sheriff**: see page 13.

*The King to the Sheriff of Kent*

*In their games, the people of our realm at one time used to practise the skill of archery, which was of great help to us – with the favour of God – in wars. Nowadays people amuse themselves with stone-throwing ... or handball, or football, or hockey, or cock-fights ... with the result that the kingdom is short of archers... We order that in all towns and villages in your county... everyone must learn and practise the skill of archery, and in his games use bows and arrows, or cross-bows and bolts... And we forbid anyone – on pain of imprisonment – to involve themselves with these other sports and pastimes, which have no use.*

Edward III, c. 1370-75

One writer prefers fishing to any other pastime.

*At the very least, he'll have the relaxation of a healthy cheering walk amongst sweet-scented herbs and flowers... He'll hear the tuneful singing of birds. He'll see young swans and cygnets following their parents, and ducks, coots, herons, and many other birds with their broods. It all seems much better to me than all the noise of hounds and the blasts of horns and the din that falconers and hunters and fowlers make. And then if the angler catches his fish, there is no man happier.*

Anon, 14th century

# Timeline

**William the Conqueror (1066-87)**[1]

*Sept 1066* William of Normandy lands at Pevensey. Defeats Harold at Hastings.

*Dec 1066* Crowned king.

*1071* William defeats English rebels at Ely.

*1085* Domesday Book survey begun.

*1087* William I killed campaigning against French.

**William II (1087-1100)**

*1091-97* William campaigns in France, Wales and Scotland.

*1096* First Crusade begins.

*1100* William II killed hunting in New Forest.

**Henry I (1100-1135)**

*1107* Early trade guild set up in Burford, Oxfordshire.

*1116-19* Henry I campaigning in France.

*1120* Heir to throne drowned when the White Ship wrecked.

*1126* Matilda, Henry's daughter, recognized as Lady of England.

*1135* Henry I dies in France.

**Stephen (of Blois) and Matilda (1135-1154)**

*1135* Stephen crowned king.

*1136* Welsh revolt against Norman colonists.

*1139* Civil War begins.

*1141* Matilda claims throne — Stephen taken prisoner, and released.

*1146* Second Crusade.

*1148* Matilda flees England.

**Henry II and Queen Eleanor of Aquitane (1154-1189)**

*1154* Henry II king. He also rules Normandy, Anjou and Aquitaine.

*1158-63* Henry in France.

*1162* Thomas Becket becomes Archbishop of Canterbury.

*1163* Rebellions in Wales.

*1166-70* Henry in France.

*1170* Murder of Becket.

*1174* Henry does penance for murder of Becket.

*1189* Third Crusade begins.

*1190* Jews robbed and killed in East Anglia and York.

**Richard I (1189-1199)**

*1193* Richard captured in France.

*1199* Richard dies of wounds fighting in France.

**John (1199-1216)**

*1204* John loses Normandy.

*1208* After quarrel with John, Pope bans Church services in England.

*1215* Sealing of Magna Carta.

*1216* Conflict with Scots.

*1215-16* Rebellions in East Anglia and Wales – John dies. Church services officially resume.

**Henry III (1216-1272)**

*1230* Henry III campaigning in France.

*1237* 'Parliament' summoned.

*1241* Henry campaigning in Wales.

*1264-65* Henry in conflict with barons.

*1264* Battle of Lewes, Henry defeated.

*1265* Parliament in London, Battle of Evesham. Henry regains power.

**Edward I (1272-1307)**

*1275* First customs duty on export of wool and leather.

*1284* Wales comes under the control of England.

*1290* Law expelling Jews from England.

*1294* Edward takes control of wool trade.

*1296* Edward invades Scotland, takes Scone.

*1297* Scots under Wallace defeat

1. Dates in brackets indicate reign of monarch.

English, invade Cumberland.
*1300* Truce with Scots.
*1305* Wallace caught and executed.
*1307* Bruce defeats English.
**Edward II (1307-1327)**
*1314* English defeated by Scots at Bannockburn.
*1315-17* Ruined harvests.
*1323* Truce with Scots.
*1327* Assembly of barons force Edward to abdicate. He is later murdered in Berkeley Castle.
**Edward III (1327-1377)**
*1338* French fleet attacks Portsmouth and Southampton.
*1340* Navy battle of Sluys, Flanders – French defeated. Edward assumes title of King of France.
*1346* Battle of Crecy – England defeats French army.
*1347* Calais filled with English colonists.
*1348-49* The Black Death.
*1351* Wages fixed at pre-Black death rates.
*1355-56* Black Prince raiding and burning towns in France.
*1360* Treaty of Bretigny between France and England.
*1361* Plague breaks out again.
*1362* Use of English ordered in law-courts.
*1362* William Langland begins to write *Piers Plowman*.
*1377* Parliament grants poll-tax of 4d per head.
**Richard II (1377-1399)**
*1381* Peasants' Revolt. Tyler killed, Ball executed.
*1387* Chaucer begins *Canterbury Tales*.
*1399* Rebellion led by Bolingbroke, future Henry IV. Richard tricked and captured, forced to abdicate.

*1400* Richard murdered in Pontefract Castle.
**Henry IV (1399-1413)**
*1400* Rebellions in Scotland and Wales.
**Henry V (1413-1422)**
*1415* Battle of Agincourt – English victory over French.
*1420* Henry marries daughter of French king.
**Henry VI (1422-1471)**
*1450* French defeat last English army to be sent to Normandy.
*1450-1471* War of the Roses.
*1461* Henry defeated, Edward IV crowned.
*1465* Henry captured and imprisoned in the Tower.
*1470* Henry restored to throne – Edward leaves.
**Edward IV (1461-1470, 1471-1483)**
*1471* Edward returns, takes London. Henry murdered in the Tower.
**Edward V (1483)**
*1483* Edward and his brother murdered in Tower.
**Richard III (1483-1485)**
*1485* Richard III defeated at Battle of Bosworth by Henry Tudor.
Henry Tudor becomes King Henry VII in 1485.

# Index